HUMAN-GHOST HYBRID PROJECT

HUMAN-GHOST HYBRID PROJECT

CAROL GUESS AND DANIELA OLSZEWSKA

Black
Lawrence
Press

Black
Lawrence
Press

www.blacklawrence.com

Executive Editor: Diane Goettel
Book and Cover Design: Amy Freels
Cover Art: Nick Marshall, from the series *From Then Until Now*, 2010

Published 2017 by Black Lawrence Press.
Printed in the United States.

Contents

The Passenger Seat of Your Car, Barreling Down Lakeshore Drive

I am only half-participating in this conversation about the Renaissance Faire strike. Both my brains have been working overtime to make me look like someone you could fall, then stay, in love with. It's exhausting, always gluing glitter animal shapes to my face. Sorry my taste in music embarrasses you. I'll make up for it by trying to look lost like you like. You cut off an undercover law van, swerve against curves, cut corners into paper dolls: long string of high femme or holiday lights eyeing crosshatched lake. I keep pressing the brake like I'm driver-decider. When you screech to a winter halt, you stretch your arm across my chest, more makeshift air bag than making out. I take what I can get while you accelerate, racing late geese and underpaid Santas jostling for the Polar Bear Plunge.

The Other Centralia

We packed Aquatic Invasive Species in suitcases and drove through the minor cities changing our safe word. You pasted stick figures to the back of the car:

girl-stick

girl-stick

fish

fish

water-moth

There's an absence of endings in a city of nightlights. Children shake cartoonishly large hands at bad drivers, eyes glazed from the dashboard telly. Two kinds of ashes fall from the sky:

fire-wag

grit-smolder

We end up in Oregon. How did we end up in Oregon again? Here's *A Book of Common Mistakes*:

untying the wrong man's shoe

putting seafeather pillows in the wash

eating snack foods with someone else's fins

tying purple seafeathers into your rough red braid

This road ends with a gift shop. We're out of cash, but they're willing to take a personal check. So many names we might forge:

Hairspray Jones

Eileen Myles

Onward Christian Soldier

Tom Waits V

Immigrant Trout

Susan

Swimming Thru a Rough Patch

If there's a motel in the back of the gift shop, we'll stay there 'til morning. Not sleeping off the miles, just filling the tub with ice from the machine down the hall.

Hypochondriac Ex-Nurse

This room smells very elderflower and hospice-afternoon. My
forehead freckles. Every time I sass the thermometer, basement
mice scurry away the special blue cheese I was saving for all of our
miraculous recoveries. My tote bag's inscribed with the old
Hippocratic oath: *Life is for the loving. First, do no less.* In school, I
was the worst at finding veins. No one volunteered to be my
partner. I punctured lovers, red running from heart to syringe. *Be
My Valentine* had special meaning. My cartoon cards were popular
with boys and girls alike. You haven't seen hunger until you've seen
an arm swollen with want in the nick of goodnight. I lost license to
practice due to licentiousness. My secret's safe in hazardous waste.

Vinyl-Scented Nostalgia Candle

Glass broke up the punk scene living in my hair, barrettes and bird's
nest tangles a tattletale display. Tambourines and coffee mugs and
whirligigs: these are all birthday-related. Romance is tidying up my
extensive music collection, while boomeranging between
Birmingham, Alabama and Birmingham, England. Something in
that vinyl tree house growls with its mammal-throat. Tonight, we'll
dance until the downstairs neighbors whack the ceiling with their
ceiling-whacking cane. *Me* is pretty, but *We* is getting stuff done:
dogs sniffing the manicured lawn of the safe house. I want to tie
you up so no one abducts you and, subsequently, ties you down. It's
a myth that vampires need an invitation. Actually, humans have the
need to invite. Whoever invented cereal had a thing about
mornings. If I were a typewriter, I'd probably misplace my keys,
too.

Your Bedroom, Which Used To Be A Utility Closet

I woke up with that doe-dead feeling about you. You reminded me too much. Don't mention nostalgia to a woman holding three different kinds of flowers in her gut. You love ballerinas again. This means you will only ever like one type of rejection at a time. Outside, a January-ish whistle. Ask about how I'll get home again now that I'm too angry to blink. Ask about when you can see where we're at in a month. Don't ask about beach glass in my galoshes. I found a text message in a bottle, sand and broken glass everywhere, okay? I woke up and went missing. You reminded your alarm to chime. Don't mention pirouettes to a pole dancer; jealousy's just reckless nostalgia. You love when the mop falls in love with the broom. Your bedroom blossoms with buckets and gloves.

Human-Ghost Hybrid Project

Bipeds cruise the Embarcadero, smart phones mimicking blackbird catcalls. Wilderness libraries loan leaflets. Don't bother the girlghost ruminating under a freestanding helmet. Weather's so yesterday. We carry DIY atmosphere in sequined totes: evensong streaked thornbruise and batblur. Wednesdays are Forest's Night Out: swag bags with bread bag lanyards for naming animals. How else to puzzle foxes from sloths, water moccasins from tawny owls? We're half-human, half-disappeared. Wind blows out our candles before we've even baked cake. There's a man I need to see about a fourth horse skull. Flexed my spooky triceps in the nature preserve behind the mortuary. The sheriff suspects, but since when does anybody listen? Autumnal in post-Ophelia dress, here's my bug-repelling spray paint spraying out of pierced nostrils. How pagan, how circa 1994. Lovely, it's okay if you're artistic and/or aphrastic. We can publish under your faux-heritage name: Wildflower Something. Your handwriting is nearly as legible as genius. Hope those horn bumps you're sporting will stay put for a month or two.

Dandy. Lion. O Dandy. (Fur)

O Lion of us, around us, haloed in sparkler-riot: flicker-bud, fat
wad of gunning gum bat bound into a hat for stem. Seeds spraying
loves me/loves me not. Hot-headed pop uncorked, umbilical for
greeny growers, mute and mother-loded. Blown glass blown out. O
Dandy animal/vegetable/mineral plucked from manicured grass,
scheduled for chemical removal bimonthly: bye. Pollination system
runs a change of pace on us. Shadow of a fur ball is lovely la la la,
my grandparents are gardeners, my grand ego has an old age
problem. Life weeds the pretty off their faces. The previous
residents were allergic. They buried their exotic dead seeds
shallowly; now the ghosts won't leave anything greened.

Parking Garage Pastoral

Leaves fall onto train wrecks and triage. We're jumpy these days, squandering our middle names on bad mortgages. Don't say they didn't warn us, although we don't know who "they" are. Warnings come with a trumpet and metallic cologne: summons rolled pre-baton and handed over post-sex, post-house painting. We should be scared, but we're eating cake from the last gay wedding we crashed in a golf cart. We've learned to wear helmets and crochet our own seat belts. We've learned a lot of things, like terms for sharpening or co-sharing a toothbrush.

I'd Forgotten How Much I Hate The Taste of Most Foods I Haven't Tried Before

You are orange and molecular and eccentrically proportioned against the slow motions of the Baltimore airport. I am Protestant-worn, waiting in an expensive restaurant, pretending to enjoy this Bloody Mary-flavored fishcake.

My stomach twists itself unconscious. You will get here eventually to report that the plane was filled with lovely and interesting people. Pat-downs go best in latex-free gloves.

Through the tear in my suitcase, my clothes look estranged. My body no longer wears that kind of waistband. I'm still dressing bite wounds. My bad for kissing a drug-sniffing dog.

In the post-9/11 waiting corral, you offer me pretzels, gnashing the foil. It's like we're in a band again, that noise, I say, but we were never those kind of girls.

Inconsequential Laboratory

What's a vice versa? The very first owl in existence probably had low self-esteem. When the universe ends, something will come along and make another universe. I left the beaker full of funeral fumes on our lovely assistant's table. A closed-circuit television shows me what effects electrodes have on these robotic strawberries. Our brains were washed, but now they're drying. Our hands misplace hand-me-down syringes, unhinged diseases hooked on kitsch. Activists smash glass and unlatch cages: stuffed animals vajazzled with crystals. Here's a herd of plush ponies running amok in our one-horse town. We need an angel investor to fund Round Six, the round where we win lollipops and faxed copies of Darwin's autograph. We're drowning in data, clowns packed into a Yellow Cab circling one-way streets, all bulbous feats and misplaced memos from the FDA.

Hot Yoga Studio

We flick slick hair from steamy glasses, give good mirror with
purloined glances. Nobody remembers which animal we're on:
Buttered Camel or Seasick Turtle? The instructor's perfecting
Microbial Mule. Upside down and out the window, Bible software
techs sport badges on the clock, off-campus.

SEAN's eating ice cream with a plastic spoon. MARSHA asks for
extra mayo.

The sky sends an alarm when lunch hour's up.

SEAN hasn't failed to notice that SARA never asks him what he's
thinking in their motel bed. There's a reason someone will only
meet you during regular business hours and that reason might well
explain the popularity of vampires.

MARSHA says don't stress so much about that extra fat rolled up
your sleeve. It's winter: everyone's kindly gone a little bit blind. Just
keep up with your flexibilities, SARA thinks. Often, I have the
opposite problem.

Travelogue Accoutrements

One of us gapes funhouse glass.

One of us is lined with silk.

One of us snaps shut as sleep.

We battle over what to tote: who carries shoes, who carries slips. Lipstick and bourbon stain moth-bitten mouths. Coal crashes as our train chugs out.

Are we yours? Our memory for faces fades with meadowlarks and lakes.

We're wary of your gloved grasp. You might belong to us, or pose strangertheftabduction danger, unsnapping us all wrong and rough.

Begone: we bite, lock zigzag jaws.

Don't pretend you're not trying to get us manhandled, we can make hitchhiking uncomfortable in this weather.

Tiny mirror in one of our middles for beauty mole check.

Nice girls go nowhere. Actually, most girls go nowhere, but our luggage tag is cut continental, and we have most of an atlas memorized like it's still school in session.

This July zips and zaps, most of your pricier unmentionables melted down travel-size.

No airport hysterics, please!

Lady, you have no idea how slow a slow boat to Show Time! actually goes.

Fine Art Of Shadow Smear

Every time I try to sext, I send photos of the body politic to my interns in Alaska. Each skirt signs *O* for Overnight. I add an *X*, thumb poised to hex. My neighbor's novel unravels on fence fronds. I shouldn't be thinking of re-gifting my kids. Wake me up when we tax the rich, or at least give everyone equal lap time with Santa. I'm putting this poem on speakerphone now. My hands obey a higher power. Mary, let's call this one *Still Life with Tangerine and Gun*. It was the perfect picture, but it kept falling off the wall every time we opened the front door. Mostly, it's too boring to go visiting your friends with feelings. Last week, though, I was tempted to motorbike out to Corpus Christi. It's August, and most of the country leans desert. When I first met Tim, he said, "You don't look anything like what I'd thought. I mean, Christopher told me that you were into politics and things like that."

Rolling Bridge

The embouchure of the architecture brilliants me while I'm rolling
along red balloon in-skirt style. Skates skitter over rickety
boardwalk. More hedgehog than giraffe, I slide over bridge
reinvented as wheel. Whatever's inside rushes up my head. Roar,
then roar again. It's all leptons vs. quarks in there. My sneaks
choose skyloft over dirt. Gulls sluice my skirt, chafing gape-jawed
fish past hem-turned-necklace. How brash of me to bride my
bridge: sky for borrowed, clouds for blue. If only you hadn't hinted
that the anti-nausea syrup's three quarters placebo. Must you bust
every flying metropolis? This city's really beautifully planned. I
mean, what did it ever do to you?

Superstition Sale

On Sundays, we set up a fort and sell wind-up woodland animals painted to look like moral imperatives. Let's try and sustain our autumnal wet-fruit-wrapped-in-hair smells. We aren't hapless; we just dress this way so people will give us a little less guidance. On Mondays, we scrap whatever's unsold: usually crows and tube-nosed bats and wind-up foxes. We junk their parts for baby seals. No one wants black cats' eyes or boys raised by wolves.

Overcoming The Ick Factor

Porcelain crankbox girl turned outside-in, you folkpop out your slippery eyes for castanets. You're a doll best loved under oldworlde kitsch code; you're a doll better loved gloved. Who sent you minus a return address? Gift horseplay for my half-birthday, no pineapple cake. Half-joke, half-threat, you remind me of Grandma's knickknacks: potpourri-stuffed doll mattresses in germanique with pinkgut, blonde-eyed girls collecting blue. Once I was you: mute and zombie-dressed, display knife turning in my back, head on a shelf, shell of myself. O princess, which collector of dance figures knows who cut out your eyes? Did you cry until they fell into your own hands? O, your maker makes a mess of dancers and dolls and zombie-gutted girls like you, but the mess can be tuneful once you take it off the shelf.

Power Nap Pillow (in neutral beige)

Vacate small talk for its shuteye variance. Hide tenderness in coat
sleeve crevice. Consider your ostrich posture a timeshare ether.
Spinning into downtime post-cubicle cringe crunch. Floaters frizz
blind spots. You're daydreamy gauze: blonde beaches, lime
margaritas, and post-feral dolphins. No one makes you root canal
the daily mail or shred volatile day planners with mortar and pestle.
Claim the Reiki you deserve! Go solo post-coital. The glass ceiling's
tufted in solar. Count the pores on the giant emoticon face that
happens along after lunch. If shoulder pads ever come back in
season, you can rest your head on those. Some turquoise dots linger
in your eyecorners. There's no such thing as failure to divorce leisure
and paycheck. We mean, why would you want anything less?

Imaginary Illustrations For Future Architecture

The silhouettes gossip in Helvetica, gathering around the eco-kettle. Krill-packed seagulls figure-eighting overhead remind me of the problems caused by glass. There's no puff along the higher angles. Rhetorically, I'm sterile as an afternoon glove. It could happen that fish relapse back into any body of water. I'm simultaneously psyched and sober. I'm simultaneously sheep and pleather. Coppice swarmed from sheet metal and linen, curtains billowing with e-card precision, my Murphy bed's trussed to a windstorm, stonefroth the soundtrack to *Daily Cottage Life & Industry*. The porch breaks it off with the topiary doe. Wasps fester under its metallic sweater.

3-D Subprime Open House

Beneath the wrecking ball, we crown visitors with candy necklaces. Pinky promise to swim the canal, bikini tops busty with sand and mirage. It's free admission Friday, daily discounts for politicians and lesbian nuns. Fresh hand towels and the artificial smell of cookies make zombie bankers frisky. Clients rave about the complimentary Tarot, sign illegible hoax signatures in the guest log. Test the soil's ph levels. Test for the more laced and pasted plagues among us. We offer tutorials in toxic assets and southwestern precocity. The trouble properties. Midwestern models arrive (gun optional). Please pay attention to our pain, which is drier and more frightening than your pain. Macrowaves make the heart grow fonder. Cue the riot against the current regime setting off our sweat glands again. The cactus is fiddling, challenging us to a duel with a devil we don't even believe in. We're scientifically recording all of this. These blueprints, they're marvelous.

Who Needs Stairs When You Have Slides?

Upward mobility as fugly affliction.

Itsy bitsy spiders make better pets and examples.

O, see our reluctant redesign of playgrounds propped up inside houses haunted by hooded insects. They needed to lose their 20th century physics.

We maximize traction, throw out more pairs of shoes than Spain knows what to do with. Swallow teaspoons whole to keep our weight under the price of silver. And yet, our cars loom large as barnyard brawls.

O cows amassing gassy balloons, bursting earth's atmospheric chandelier!

O electric shredder, crinkling mortgages and overdues and oops— pink diary's locked tooth!

Getting Awkward With The On And Off

You stare at a video loop of lightning bolts striking black and white cows like it's the first sex tape you've ever seen.

Power down for summer pause, Autotime in lieu of Starstutter.

You don't need a power source; cruise control is in the eye of the beholder.

The museum's solar panel sneaks a peek at your widow's peak.

Off duty, yet dutiful, the security guard flashlights through the freshly-vacuumed Hallway of Statues Wearing Sunscars.

He nightshifts because he's covered in carcinogenic triangles.

He's covered in carcinogenic triangles because college turned out to be expensive.

College turned out to be expensive because STEM fields and/or the History of Western Art.

Girlbox For Sale

Shrink yourself small enough to sell. As product, you're proud packaging. Placement's a blur of aesthetics and finance. Customers prefer objects located eye level on up. No one kneels anymore; new knees cost gold. Your contents clutter the sides of the box: heart, hands, flash-bosom, lip liner, rust. You taste like seashells and pink candy necklace. Small children finger your cellophane sweater. Nutritionists marvel at potassium levels. No high fructose corn syrup here, just Polaroids and gum. The rabble's roused, fetches a geode to wrap around your little finger. Let them sniff your tight and festively-curled hair, then upgrade to glass display case with combination lock. The manager keeps asking if it's not all wasted on the likes of you. Blush violent, blush until it's purpling flowerings all the way up to your scalp. Humble yourself in calico. Offer to be every Michigander's bridesmaid. Paradox: the more you try to appease, the angrier the royal *We* gets. Crochet flowers, memorize Latin prefixes, keep from wanting much of anything strange or difficult. Pick something to be good at and do that until you forgive or forget the first three-fourths of your life on the sob shelf.

Every Diver Has A Dumpster Story

The stalagmites gleamed upwards out of the old bin and the city sky turned that paper brown shade. Empty chairs took to gathering in circles. Loungers and swivel-backs rubbed legs like they were used to rude apocalypses. Small bushes burned out before anyone could turn their words into medicine, the mechanism for keeping a tongue well past out of fashion. Bleak-mouthed, it was at least as bad as suspected. First hands, then hoards of climbers clambered over the dumpster's metallic teeth. Syringes stabbed Styrofoam to-go husks. Deflated mattresses undressed for sex. Some shabby chic gilt replaced a live oak, dead at the root. Everyone blamed hoarding on family of origin: decades of pre-internet newsprint piled sky high in studio apartments.

Art Sick

I popped a balloon for the sake of a funny thing to say at the next
fabulous thing-saying event. My art is full of natural disasters. I
whistled a map of music, photographed a girl in red muttonchops.
At the show, we stood on the flattest robots. I asked everyone if
they didn't like my earlier work better. Licked the right people in
the wrong corners. I made art from milk and the girl drank it down.
It was more experimental than conceptual. My name on a banner
blinking her mood. Someone was opening my snail mail by then,
stalking circa 1992.

Back To The Cornmaze

Every tractor has a mother, an even bigger tractor tearing into cornsilk with her teeth. Repeat after me: *No U-Pick Pumpkins.* Someone always gets hurt among the prickly vines. It would be easier for you if I was ruthless. Because I'm basically nice, this part is hard. Let's think more on tractors and a murder of crows. Yes, and a scarecrow. Think about that. Mostly, I am really bad at operating heavy machinery. When I bridged the country moon to your mouth, you flinched and I fell even further from me. Please note that I didn't do it on purpose. You hand over your shy map. Suddenly tired, I ask for permission. This is your first time shaking angrily. We might not be able to hold it together past harvest. Any omen can be terrifying in the midst of a hundred year drought.

In The Original Version They Cut Out Her Tongue

Let's talk about
the dinosaur version
of <i> Little Red Riding Hood</i>:
    Why, Grandmother, what great
    bones you have—cold and marked
    up from the meteor showers.

Let's talk about
the beauty school version
of <i> Rapunzel</i>:
    O, your shade and volume
    of blonde is so verily
    matching my needs right now.

Let's talk about
the dissociative version(s)
of <i> The Ugly Duckling</i>:
    Don't ever let reflections
    get in the way of your real
    life that you still get to live.

Let's talk about
the queercore version
of <i> Snow White</i>:
    Red lips mean Fever Forever-
    flavored gloss, gnawing
    the apple post-daintily and decorum-less.

Let's talk about
the captivity narrative version
of *The Goose Girl*:
      Changeling princess snatched
      from bus stop, photographed
      cartwheeling in the back seat of a car.

Let's talk about
the Aryan version
of *Hansel and Gretel*:
      Into the dark woods' dark
      on dark. Otherness opening
      a dark-mouthed oven.

Let's talk about
the Tea Party version
of *Cinderella*:
      Pretty, with mice, chasing gems
      in manshape. Upward mobility
      hobbled by halfshoe.

Verso Recto Refracted

This summer was supposed to be all kite parties and two-nickel
lemonade. What with my thighs chafing in seersucker boysuit and
August doing its best imitation of a housecat. But I'm not that into
drugs anymore, so there is too such a thing as an incredibly stupid
question—it polka dots all over my stomach every time you decide
to wait forever before calling me backward. I'm all frontispiece and
light frock coat, knees quaking, tugging muslin over invisible
ankles. You didn't have to rename the cat. Engraved pages of last
season's journal dangle from the shotgun stoops of Tuscaloosa.
Flytraps sticky with Karo flutter and sigh, the kind of music I'm
listening to these days.

If We Wanted A Fire, My Task Was The Kindling

There's a camp hemming down shore. Nights, they bugle post-reverie Reveille. Bad boys are for drowning: a little sigh and no one remembers his dull blonde damp. Whatever we bring burns in towns named for seabirds. Rocks lack decorum, trample new mosses: bentleaf, horntooth, haircap, beaked. Now ferry. Hold onto the railing. Once a month, someone believes she can spark. Children wish on soft plashes, swim through plate glass on off-port bows. They sweat out gills and role-play like sharks with evolutionary tendencies. Watch them weave through the kelp with optimistic firebird poses. If a phoenix drowns, its zombie takes the form of a red and orange fish. An underwater matchbook might stay hooked in a coral reef for centuries.

Thinking Of You, I Google Your Secret

Bridal shower games include: designing dresses out of gauze and guessing the number of guns in the room. Nothing I feel happens in real time. Guests strip to their skivvies and prank call the groom. You, for example, in that pineapple chair, wedding cake frosting smeared on the ottoman. Easy enough to stay uninvited: I show up minus lasso, last night in my hair. Everyone gets careful and funeral-faced. Sorry about that "anonymous" Internet tip-off. For the record, you've never struck me as an xxxxxxxxxx fetishist. Actually, I think pastels will make us more Zen, less Luddite. The Amish, you know, don't even believe in maids of honor. Yeah, this gift card? I hope it really means a lot to you and Jim.

Collaborative Divorce Lawyer's Office, Midtown

The fish tank glitters with swimmers, worn out circling the pink castle's bubbles. I'm sliding off the leather couch. I'm pacing past single serve coffee packets and unlit outdoor-scented candles. *Come in.* I do. There's room for two by two inside the stairwell, where I've found a new hobby—smoking—to replace my old hobby—knitting. I puff cold air into new years. If I were the force of nature you say I am, I'd be a tree. Instead, I'm wearing tights and flats that rub skin off my heels. I don't know what *collaborative* means. If I were a fish, I'd probably overeat. People buy mice to feed to snakes they've bought from stores that grow by the freeway. Nothing about me is good at change. When you were out of town, I didn't finish reading a fortune cookie that seemed to apply too much to our present situation. Lately, the clocks don't tock straight. They sound like they're underwater. You've started seeing how unflattering I look against the green and broken synapses. A perfectly capable hibernation strategy might let me put this off until spring, but spring is an even worse season to make our outsides match our insides. So, kiss me on my forward one last time, hand me a good pen. Let's clean up legal-like, finalize this aquarium before the birds come back.

Ancestry For Beginners

Scientists' children are unbearably attractive. Especially when they chew cigars with their orthodontics.

Artists' children are excellent secret-keepers. As long as the secrets don't involve numbers.

We showed up late to the daycare meeting wearing designer sunglasses. You were carrying a shovel; I was fiddling with the battery from the smoke detector. We brought ten Q-tips to put in the frog jars.

Also, rose-scented rope.

Children replicated themselves, family histories pinned to their coats. Their lunchbox notes begged strangers for money.

We bought flasks, cheap gin, twin tickets to spend each sixth night alone. The ceiling fan whirled naptime into an un-frenzy. "Too bad we're second cousins," pointing to the grudge I carried, a deadbeat hometown.

It Gets Harder From Here On Out

Or is it easier? We can never remember which. The winding road, abduction narrative running through my hair, wind socking bare trees: all in it to win it. I'm the prize, or maybe the referee. You're sure it's next left or is it right? We stop for smoke-flavored potatoes. The bascule bridge suffers slowly like snails. We're never crisscrossing off each other's lists or maps or High Mercury Astrology Charts. The record skips handclaps posthaste. Our love of back alleys grows in proportion to our inner GPS. It's like we're in a female road trip movie, only no one ends up driving off a cliff or signing a recording contract.

Suburban Feral

Gray cat's speaking in tongues again, praying for birds to fall from
their bowers under the neighbor's tinfoil tree. Last night's Bar-B-Q
invited me not, Americana cozies flirting with lawn chairs' distant
cousins. Music mistakenly rhymes "love" with "sick." I tugged trash
cans to the curb, microwaved salad mix and called it wilted. How to
get a dance party going solo. How to party behind a very large gate?

Harp And Underwater Flowers

There's so much Atlantic Ocean we'll have to operate even in our sleep. Thus quoteth the moon, morosely, to the ogre in a rowboat and his harp-playing dog. An anonymous passenger popped the red balloon taped to the top of his ladies' hat. The moon gave a slow groan at the ogre's once-upon-a-time face. Everyone prepared to be inspected by the coast guard. Everyone stripped off their scuba diving gear and took care not to breathe out with their mouths. The dog played Top Forty covers as the coast guard texted a report to the chief: *Dear Chief, We've got a situation that requires more birds.* Soon a regulation flock of albatrosses descended on the tiny deck, which promptly sank. Now this is an underwater-type story. Now you'll get the mermaid you've been waiting for. The mermaid you've been waiting for is very beautiful and looks nothing like a coffee logo. Her hair hangs long. It hangs swimmingly. Her girl parts glint, covered with shiny scales. You can't get in there. She isn't that kind of girl. Her tail swishes your stomach and tickles your feet.

Watering The Dead

flowers, my neighbor leans too far over the railing and loses his
footing. It would be maudlin if this wasn't so southern. Last night,
we built a fire in the fake fireplace, used our Internet stocks for
kindling. You felt all pomegranate and don't-look-back. One
Sunday, after community lawn mowing, we shared our password
selection process: the trick is to pick the same password as
everybody else, no one ever suspects their own password. We're
together now, as if the war never happened. Smart phones text
drones: *How about drinks?* Aliens emoticon from their chrome
saucers. When I pass, turn my ashes into microchips. Pyramids are
for posers. Gardens are for necrophiliacs. Next Sunday, we'll
un-locust. We'll learn to love thy fellow citizens in circles, in place
of gem-ringed roses and mourning wreaths.

Steam Knows Where We Live

Lids should be free, but they cost more than coffee. You ask for sugar; I give you three cubes. You ask for cream; I give you three cows. The cows are cow-shaped. They pour and pour. Baristas make smell talk: *top note fade out.* Art school kids poke holes in day-olds. Okay, so. Now we know what to look for.

I'm Not Staring; I Mean, I'm Not Staring At You

Avidly, you turn through the finale without setting off the fire alarm or the woman in distress alarm. Don't wink at me. I'm just rehearsing my lines silently with my eyes open like they're impressed. Purse your lips pink. Jesus, you think everyone wants to hold your hat. Plunging necklines are so pre-default. Why does each shoulder need a pocketbook with a rhinestone strap? If you corner me in Ladies', I'll unman you. No, I won't lend you my girlfriend: go heist your own. Twirl her into your chignon, angel/ devil voice perched halo-heavy. Flutter your lashes for lift-off, red rockets shooting from the soles of your kitten-heeled pumps. There's a tiny and jeweled Chupacabra with your name on its collar. There's a dead detective carrying your number scrawled on a receipt from a drugstore in Tijuana.

When I Was

Hair lost off my long navigational finger is barely noticeable.
Dimmer switches for eyelids no longer indicate communicable
disease. Western Hemisphere is what I call the bump over the top
of my hips. Anyways, brick bundles are funnier than babies. The
rubble and rabble sucked on my tired toes.

I feel guilty every time I think about how much worse you had it
swimming to school through six feet of snow.

Then I feel guilty about feeling guilty.

Then I feel pointy and then I feel flat.

Mornings, I make mirror-face while brushing my teeth. Work-face,
fun-face, sex-face, sleep-face: I'm a circus and you're the net. No,
you're a net and I'm seafloor, snared. Row that boat, baby, you say,
mean face-ed-ly.

Peak Ferry Wait Time Starts With You

Everyone's parked in line for a gawk at the islands. Let's get hush-hush with the ticket-taker and gallop backwards for coffee. Eagles roost in burnt-out streetlights shadowing the taco stand. A little salsa and we've rolled our jeans akimbo. You carry the dog past tourists taking photos of you carrying the dog. Gelato sounds wrong. But how else to encourage summer not to rush her crooked smile? Let's flagellate the paper towel dispenser until it gives us what we want: dry hands. Pink plastic pockets for lady products suggest garbage cans are cleaner than biology can handle. I'm seasick past ginger, reading map after map of why *You Are Here*.

Domesticity + Late Capitalism = Reality TV

Girl-salt, boy-salt: any way you shake it, the table's set. I don't care how much money you make, you can't go lighting flatware on fire. When the service is lousy, pretend we're in a restaurant. I'm a stranger who spilled coffee because I'm overworked, not because I love your lap and wanted to give it a day off. I mean, I love you and wanted to see if you're part-mythology, part-mermaid. I wanted to see if you'd drown. Anyways, does my apron look authentic to you? The Belgian-American actor who provides voiceover for the show worries that it does not. I heard there's going to be an egg-tossing contest. The prize is an Easter Bunny and a two-week vacation to Easter Island. Now it's time to nominate two of the remaining contestants for the neighborhood association. You say that grass-trimming and French manicures come from the same impulse: thwarted hunger for overseas adventure. Contestant #5 used to be a stripper at a pirate-themed bar. I worry about the way you look at the sound tech. I mean, I worry about the way the sound tech looks at you. At least we've all agreed not to use the word "harvest" when we talk about beheading chickens. At least we've all agreed who should get voted off the Kitchen Island.

The Sun Never Sets And Your Brother Is Almost Always Wrong

There are galaxies and they do gymnastics over the giant tree. If you manage to hang monkey around one of the smaller branches, you might glimpse a shard of sun recycled past atmosphere.

Your brother's around here somewhere, wearing a weird cut of robe. He thinks he died, but, as usual, he's sorely mistaken.

There are pretty birds. There are dead birds. Your brother is trying to tell his father and your stepfather that the birds are unable to get sick.

There's a cure for all this quasi-death, but as usual it belongs to people with money. They're uninterested in birds as a rule, confusing flamingos with origami cranes.

When your brother discourses on the afterlife, roll your eyes and get busy dusting the candelabra. You've collected so many, dripping wax in every corner. And porcelain dolls, dimples hand-carved, posed with silk flowers and bubblegum pistols.

How could you ask for another life with an ice chest full of meat and a father who loves you? Or seems to, although he misspells your name and vanishes for weeks at a time without calling. Your foremother died. She stole eggs and ate them. It isn't difficult to die this way. You think if you're given your choice of death you'll fall from a tree, not down but up.

The Freeway Is Always In Emotional Turmoil

Don't do that while I'm driving; it rips the bandage off the wound. Then we're in an ambulance instead of a taxi, excused from the responsibility of making our own siren sounds at the red light. No one in Oregon pumps their own gas. It's a law, like not threading needles on Sunday. God doesn't want you to chuff His fumes. Then the Interwebz made us in its own creature-image, thumbs grew un-opposable, were unable to oppose. Shrinking Darwins, we didn't even need to drive anyplace important. It's fine; we're not sorry, just nostalgic: driving goggles and driving gloves and driving coats lined with storkstuffs. This morning, I woke up wishing we owned two cars: one for you and one for the you who is still into that woman from Michigan. Fuck Michigan. I'm not riding around in anything to do with Michigan. I mean, I'll act adult when I feel like it. Like, even an interior decorator can remember to check the oil every other time she stops to refill the tank.

Three Sheep Make a Chair, Are Made Into a Chair

Minus chignon, shorn to sheepskin, I perched in the stylist's throne-booth and wept. Her thimble slipped, nipping my nape. What she snipped couldn't be latched; my braid fell as broomfodder, splayed on the faux marble floor.

From a perch in the corner of Salonité, a trio of sheep claimed me as kin. Unblinking eyes rolled in stiff sockets: Baby's First Taxidermy Project.

Stylist Christie pouted through product, spritzing me minty, oil to scalp.

"Hair grows out, but dead is dead."

A tripartite sheep gaze glazed my walk of shame down Main.

"Deader than a doornail, but twice as pretty."

My monthly furniture bill varies wildly, is dependent on enforcement of husbandry laws. Some say black sheep are impervious to propaganda.

Whether or not this is a police state, I want to arm wrestle, settle ownership of the herd of scrap animals resting under the maple tree. An unnatural disaster is coming. I feel it bumping behind the eyeballs of this sheep.

Princess-ish

Princess E:
Put a bloodied and purpling flower over a blue tri-corner and under a dead ostrich. Don't tremble—where are the ponies? The rice is in your handmaiden's handbag, we hope, we hope.

> Potential Prince A:
> Mustn't sneeze. Allergic
> to peonies and ostrich.
> I'm the pony you've
> been dreaming of.

Princess B:
An ovary overhead is worth two in the midsection. Earth tones are complimentary, rigorously tailored. We won't photograph you as much as you'd like.

> Potential Prince B:
> I like a woman
> who wears her genitalia
> on her head, artistically
> rendered. I wear mine
> tucked: back home, shades
> drawn, under delicate dresses.
> If you'd like a combo
> gentleman + fashionista,
> give me a ring.

Princess E:
Do you ever get nervous when everything goes right? It can't last, the feeling of stuff working from the inside out.

Potential Prince C:
Charming is my middle
section, all six-pack
abs: delight. I don't care
for you at all, just
mirrored halls, and you've
got plenty. Decades
of gilt, guilt-free.

Princess B:
Ask us how we went about spending our summers, it has nothing to
do with sailing, we promise.

Potential Prince D:
How about a rowboat?
Day-old bread, pockets
inside out, plaid
lining bright as gold?
Must you marry money?
I break beats
like wicked royalty.

Pocket M

We're all gussied up in street cred, socks color-coded to match each other's synesthesia. Sometimes you text me by accident, whole sentences scripted by jacket pocket: *straight-acting big pharma cuttlefish tome.* Now I know where I left my glasses and why you tossed flowers from the getaway car. The bank slithered away behind us, *Just Married.* Guards fired rice. A teller caught your bouquet. I'm wearing pinstripes over pajamas in honor of Thursday being the new Friday. When a car flashes its brights, I put on more clothes. Your white dress got hitched to Silly Putty and string cheese. It melts as we roll up the windows and sing. We've got a little Bonnie and Clyde left in our mouths. We've got a little Dillinger metal left in our chests. I want what you're wearing. Nobody's ever asked me for my favorite bedtime story before. If I loved you any less, I'd have already told you about what happened in Atlantic City. We can still get there in time for fashionably late. Our courthouse date was definitely over-attended. I was surprised at the number of protesters with birdcages balanced atop their heads. The judge is not amused. He said that, really, this could have been a quiet affair. It didn't need to turn into the kind of thing that might ruin your dad's chance at the party's nomination.

Eyelet And Eyesore

The boss said *prenup*, not *pre-need*.

Here I am, married to my job again.

Sometimes a girl just has to wear white, trip over her veil on the way to HR.

The honeymoon was downsized off yachts overlooking offshore accounts.

It isn't easy being smarter than Marketing or negotiating a rainbow-colored parachute without a ripcord.

Even my dress dressed down on casual Friday, leaving me unlaced and French-cut in the breast pumping closet.

We downed corporate coffee on company time ("we" meaning "me and peeps at my pay grade").

We passed notes in infrared ("we" meaning "the two secretaries from Legal").

My dowry was ivy-covered, everyone meant for me to wed up.

Every Halloween, I costume in a new First World Problem.

I love my ability to love whatever loves me back, it makes me stay slim enough to look good in lace.

All day long, I've been surfing the web for vintage jewelry. My best friend from college wanted to be an astronaut. I don't know whether or not I should send her this link about the planet they just discovered: it's made entirely out of diamonds, it's like four thousand light years away.

Business Casual

I am my own worst seamstress, altering publicly and impulsively, scissoring indiscriminately through ten or more yards of pinstripes and discreet diamond prints. You come to my defense, assure horrified onlookers that I'm not usually this slutty, it's only since I shrank too short to wear off-the-rack. Last night, a cop dropped me off in the parking lot of Tuscaloosa's FEMA trailer department store. My face was painted to look like one of the Mesozoic Era's smaller dinosaurs. You acted like you were happy to see me. We linked arms and skipped over to our boss' party: croquet on the lawn with a Green Beret. My boa (fake feathers in love with real birds) wound itself around a banister. You hobnobbed after too many spritzers and kissed someone's wife in the pantry; I know. In the car, I scalloped my hem with the ice scraper I bought in Chicago. Sequins detached and measled the gas. It's easy to accessorize with fossil fuels.

Hotel Lobby, U District, Big Game Starts at Five

A balloon flotilla floats above flat fee parking. *Leave your car with us we know how to love.* Sext photos of joke hotdogs from a car-turned-cart overturned on the Ave. *She who fails to love face paint* deserves to park six stories under team colors. Alumni abandon wheel lives, fall for cheerless leaders struggling with self-esteem. *It's hard to get tossed and come down perfume* you wouldn't wish on your uncle's first wife. It's easy to holiday under this weather. We worry about the gift baskets, though. Every other letter embroidered redly over our chests: *Go Temp!* Is this really what we spent sleepless through December for? A socially acceptable reason to obscene at people in wrong-colored hats? This is a rich Saturday dish: a $200 catalyst warms its center. Compliments to the undertaker; compliments to the chef. Let's do this again next year? Same time, same place?

Flotation Devices

Snakes swim with their heads above water, lake garbage-green and
fish-nippled. I'm lounging on this blown-up flower, you're lounging
on that blown-up clown. Sunrays break into semesters. I'm not
scared of sewer disease, this heat feels so sufficiently antiseptic.
Balm autocorrects *sunburn* to *sunbeam*. You blink or bruise easily:
which is it, and why are we in Michigan when the quake's in DC?
We circle-talk the moving in together situation, this August really
needs to start ending soon. Corporate sponsors logo our waterpolo
weedwack togas. Time to unpack our gaydar for girl names of
hurricanes-slash-tropical storms.

Still Life With Two-Way Mutual Non-Disclosure Agreement

I thought I'd vacuumed the cat, but it was just a fur shadow game of left behind. The sky's pink. We're getting our goodnight on. You open the windows so the neighbors will know. In the sitcom version, our family's surname begins with B. No one sneezes or chooses wrecked-heart. In the version I live in, cat vamps hello with a felt stub for a tongue. The table's raw leg rocks on. I'm losing confidence in the right things to know. We've got poison and/or animal control on speed dial. My capacity to remain entertained is infinite. Blink once and it's half past three am, eyes swole up to hospital size. There's no such thing as pet allergies, you say, or bisexuals. Okay, maybe it's almost light enough to go walk around by the east docks. We need to work us out a new don't-ask policy, one that will hide the bald on all our femme parts.

Oath In The Direction Of Arbitrary

You are super sped up, two miles away from blurring. My
grandmother used to make us wear coats in the middle of June,
said she got chills looking at our bare arms. I'm getting nauseated
trying to look at your whole body at once. You are fat with
hummingbirds hiding bullets in their beaks. We do a lot, but it's
still not even a fraction of what you think we could be doing. If I
was less slow, we'd already be done re-alphabetizing my spice rack.
You get nauseated trying to focus in on just one part of my body.
I'm fat with sea slugs bearing garlands of poppy seeds. Your
grandmother made you wear food you couldn't finish: buttersmear
brassieres and split pea stoles. Together, we litter the condiment
aisle with promises typeset in invisible ink. We get dizzy trading
glasses for fashion's sake, my near-sloth for your far-mania.
Nostalgia happens when we least expect it, before we store two
weeks' worth of water and a month's worth of beans in the cellar
beneath the neighbor's son's second wife's second house. No one
thinks to look for our stash of childhood anecdotes and infectious
diseases, baby shoes worn to nubs from your running away skill set.
Mine are bronzed, squat among knick-knacks. We're so much alike
no one remembers my name.

Difficulties Encountered While Trying to Reenact 'The Swimmer'

The difference between swimming in your swimsuit and swimming in your underwear is only arbitrary until the apartment complex's security guard shows up with the world's biggest flashlight and starts asking weird questions about our tastes in star signs. When we ran into those people I'm currently not speaking to ever again, I was at least wearing a towel. It used to be that everyone worried about cramping, cramping could be avoided by never eating less than twenty minutes before getting in. It used to be that everyone worried about the man who came to clean the pool. He told me that the last time he was arrested, nuns threw a party for bail money. Night swimming works best if you glow in the dark, skin lit by an energy drink, the kind that sets your innards flashing. You're neon pink, I'm neon blue; together we're the peculiar shade of orange that rhymes with everything. The difficulty of reenacting the canon is girl parts above the automatic vacuum that sucks up plastic ducks each year. We're not suburban enough for critics to rub sunscreen on the tender spots behind our knees. If we've got wives, they're in the bathhouse, ogling.

Lullaby for the Shenanigans

Don't fall into prey drive in front of the vestibule grande.

There's no room for splayed legs or clinical trials.

Your hedgehog graffiti is all over this motel receipt.

Present raw bits and wrong bits, explain why those pink-tipped things don't quite cut it: paisley the bedspread, plug-in carnie toys, help mix cotton candy flavor with spirit flavor.

If there's a countdown, be the minute hand's version of Easy Listening while you soap. Be the rubbed down coastline in the above-bed watercolor.

Wrap yourself in a bloodless semi-opaque shower curtain.

Your REM is atonal, but the décor appeals to your latent sense of regeneracy.

Influence rudimentary feathers around your head.

Alarm yourself, the opposite of a wake-up call.

Let's Devil In The Details

or maybe the mail. Let's make a new version of Facebook, call it Bookface. Let's give each other nicknames that sound like knacknames. Let's kiss crows yielding butchery bits mixed with Styrofoam seeds. Let's learn to knit out of spite. Let's pratfall instead of prankcall, take up twin speak, become the talk of Flood Street. Let's scuba dive downtown, shoplift pancakes and syrup packets. Let's queen, leave cut hair in beggar bowls, paint our lips low-residency red, tie sugar sacks to the backs of political and romantical effigies. Let's horn and tail, burn and wah wah wail. Let's all this, let's much much more. Let's dance, though our feet be gumstuck to the floor.

The Details Of My Yes

Consider the two-step conditioning. Private combinations of heel-toe, heel-toe make do in the velvet-vulgar dance halls of Chicago. It took me a while to recognize that your foot had an accent. My encyclopedia of expressions sass minor-keyed. Jazz rolled in one ear and never came out the other, balance always off, something for flappers to quip brightly about. These poison-colored shoes aren't tickets to places with showcases. No one notices our sapphire perfume or silver mascara. Our necklines natter on about necklaces. Hemlines argue about leaving home. What's a pocket flask got to do with girl parts and how much gin does it take to flash an anklet? I'm undecided about everything but my next tattoo. You're decisive about everything but when to stop traffic. Midnight comes back each time we think we've banished "Good Day!" Some clock hands don't know when to say no. You fire the starter. I *pas de bourrée* and *pirouette*. Friends place bets on which way this will go.

Crab Cake Walk

Vertically gowned, lake-bound, a billion fish disprove the last leaden hook theory. Underwater, but still overland, pirate gold pockets incur sea goddess wrath. Hence, dead pirate face; hence, unlikely accommodations in the mermaids' gated community. Password: *Fin*. How will you know which "I" I am when I'm fickle, changing gown to gun to guardrail? How will you know which stain to choose: splayed legs or lips? Which tilts the earth back on its axis after earthquake, tornado, and man-made disaster? We're doing swimmingly down here, sans online shopping and Tea Party celesbians. Introverted whales spout off. We flick our tails, scales bright as stolen cigarettes. We wait for shipwrecks.

Acknowledgments

Carol and Daniela would like to thank their friends and family.

Special thanks to Nick Marshall for the front cover photograph.

Special thanks to all at Black Lawrence Press.

Carol Guess is the author of sixteen books of poetry and prose, including *Doll Studies: Forensics* and *Tinderbox Lawn*. In 2014 she was awarded the Philolexian Award for Distinguished Literary Achievement by Columbia University. Her most recent book, *With Animal*, was co-written with Kelly Magee and published by Black Lawrence Press. She teaches in the MFA program at Western Washington University.

Daniela Olszewska is the author of four other collections of poetry and short prose, including *cloudfang : : cakedirt* (Horse Less Press) and *Citizen J* (Artifice Books).